CHRISTMAS

COOKBOOK

Marilyn Bright

ILLUSTRATED BY BRIDGET FLINN

KEY PORTER BOOKS

First Published in 1992 by
The Appletree Press, Ltd
19–21 Alfred Street, Belfast BT2 8DL

Published in Canada by:

Key Porter Books Ltd
70 The Esplanade
Toronto, Ontario
Canada M5E 1R2

Canadian Cataloguing in Publication Data

Bright, Marilyn
The Christmas cookbook

(The Little Kitchen collection)
Includes index.
ISBN: 1-55013-423-X

1. Christmas cookery. I. Title. II. Series.
TX739.2.C45B75 1992 641.5'68 C92-094520-1

Printed and bound in the E.C.

92 93 94 95 96 5 4 3 2 1

Introduction

Christmas memories are about the scent of crushed pine needles, the glow of candlelight on snow-framed windows, and the warmth and fragrances radiating from the heart of the house – the kitchen. For those who love Christmas, the pleasures of busy preparation are part of what the great day is about. The spicy smells of baking, the great stirrings-up, the chopping and the peeling make the cook's kingdom the center of attraction for family and friends.

The recipes in this little book are distilled from Christmases in many different places, in times past and present. Our Christmas plum pudding has changed little since it was handwritten into a medieval lady's "receipt" book. Its spiky holly decoration comes from an even older tradition, meant to keep away evil spirits. The glorious flaming arrival of the pudding reminds us of the Child who came to bring light to the world. Today's cooks carry on these traditions and forge a direct link to Christmases past and all those to come.

Roast Goose with Apple, Prune, and Potato Stuffing

It was the triumphant arrival of the golden roasted Christmas goose that caused the Cratchit family such delight in Dickens' *A Christmas Carol.* At its succulent best during midwinter, goose was the traditional holiday centerpiece long before turkey arrived to dominate Christmas tables. Its rich fattiness is best complemented by sharp and sweet fruit flavors as in Germany, where goose is served with apples, prunes, and sweet-sour red cabbage.

1 goose, 10–14lb, dressed weight
1 bouquet garni: *parsley, bay leaf, thyme*
2 tbsp butter
4 cups chopped onions
3 large celery stalks with tops, chopped
3 cups thinly sliced tart apples
4 scant cups cooked mashed potato
grated rind of 1 lemon
1 cup softened prunes, chopped
1 tsp ground mace
salt, pepper
1–2 tbsp flour
Serves 6-8

Clean goose and scrub inside and out with salt. Put neck and giblets into a pan with water and *bouquet garni*; simmer for 1½–2 hours to make stock. To make stuffing, melt butter in a large pan and sauté onions, celery, and apples until soft. Combine with mashed potato, lemon rind, and chopped prunes. Season with mace, salt, and pepper.

When mixture is cold, stuff loosely into goose cavity. Prick goose skin all over with sharp fork or skewer, place on rack in an uncovered pan and put into oven preheated to 450°F. After 10

minutes, reduce heat to 350°F and cook for 15 minutes per pound, including stuffing weight. Test for doneness by pricking thickest part of thigh near the body and making sure juices have no tinge of pink.

When goose is cooked, make gravy by pouring off all but 2 tablespoons of fat from roasting pan and stirring in flour. Blend in strained stock from giblets, heat until thickened, and season to taste.

Rillettes

This rich pâté, long a favorite at holiday gatherings in the pork-rearing regions of France, is spread on crusty bread and accompanied by the local wine. It can also be made with a proportion of goose, duck, or rabbit meat.

2lb boneless pork belly
8oz pork fat
1 tbsp salt
1 clove garlic, crushed
grated nutmeg
freshly ground black pepper
1/4 cup water
Makes 2 lbs

Cut the pork belly and pork fat into 3/4 inch cubes, sprinkle with salt and leave covered overnight. Next day, transfer to a heavy-bottomed pan, put in the remaining ingredients, cover and cook very gently over low heat or in a low oven for at least 4 hours, until the meat is falling apart and stewing in the released fat. Strain over a large bowl and allow excess fat to drain off. Using two forks, shred the meat to make rough pâté. Correct seasoning if necessary, pack into sterilized earthenware bowls or jars, and seal with a layer of the melted reserved fat.

Oyster Stew

Fish and seafood often figured in the Christmas Eve feast in the days when religious observance forbade meat before the great day. Spiced carp features in Germany and Austria, pickled herring in Scandinavia. Luxurious fresh oysters find favor in France and on the east coast of the United States, where warm, buttery stew greets snow-weary travellers.

2 dozen oysters
2 tbsp butter
2 tbsp flour
3 cups milk
2/3 cup heavy cream
freshly-grated nutmeg
cayenne pepper
lemon juice
salt
butter (optional)
Serves 4

Open oysters and reserve their strained liquor. Melt butter over gentle heat and stir in flour. Gradually add milk, stir until smooth, and add cream. Allow to come to just the simmer and season with nutmeg, cayenne, and a little lemon juice. Add oysters and their liquor, taste for seasoning and add salt if necessary. Heat just until oysters are warm through and serve immediately with little pats of butter floating on top, if liked.

Chestnut and Stilton Soup

Two Yuletide treats combine to make warming soup with a Christmassy air. A good prelude to holiday feasts, this is a perfect make-ahead choice.

1lb chestnuts
1 tbsp butter
1 small onion, chopped
2 stalks celery with tops, chopped
$2^1/4$ cups turkey or chicken stock
$2^1/4$ cups whole milk
about 1 cup crumbled Stilton cheese
lemon juice
salt, white pepper
parsley
Serves 6

Using a sharp knife, cut an X in each chestnut and roast in a hot oven for about 10 minutes. Quickly peel off shell and skin before chestnuts cool. Melt butter and gently sauté onion and celery until soft. Add chestnuts, put in stock and milk and simmer for about 30 minutes, until chestnuts are very soft. Puree mixture in blender or food processor, add Stilton and puree again. Season to taste with lemon juice, salt, and pepper and reheat. Serve garnished with small parsley sprigs.

Caramel Potatoes

Sugar-browned potatoes are the Danish accompaniment to Yuletide goose, but are delicious with other roast poultry, ham, or pork. If you can't find early new potatoes, quarter large potatoes and trim into ovals.

1½ lb new potatoes
4 tbsp butter
4 tbsp sugar
salt
Serves 4

Scrub potatoes and cook until slightly underdone. Cool quickly and peel. In a heavy frying pan, melt the butter and sugar, stirring and taking care not to burn. When the mixture is a light brown caramel, lower the heat and put in potatoes, stirring to coat evenly. Transfer to heated dish and sprinkle with salt.

Carrot and Almond Pudding

Root vegetables of the long, dark winters are given festive treatment in this Finnish Christmas Eve dish. It is a main-course accompaniment rather than a sweet, and a whole almond hidden in the pudding wins the finder a special prize.

1 1/2lb carrots
4 tbsp butter
2 tbsp finely chopped onion
2 tbsp finely chopped parsley
2 tbsp flour
1 cup milk
1 1/2 tbsp brown sugar
salt, pepper
1/4 cup breadcrumbs
1/4 cup slivered almonds
Serves 5-6

Peel and cook carrots. Mash, or purée in food processor. Melt butter and gently sauté the onion and parsley. Stir in flour and gradually add milk, stirring smooth. Cook until thickened. Mix carrot purée and brown sugar. Cook for another minute or two. Season with salt and pepper and pour into a greased baking dish. Top with breadcrumbs and almonds and bake in oven preheated to 350°F for about 30 minutes.

Red Cabbage with Apples

Rich, ruby-red cabbage gleams on the Christmas table, as good to eat as it is to look at, perfect company for the holiday bird or for ham. It actually improves when made in advance.

2 tbsp butter or goose dripping
4 slices smoky bacon, diced
1 large onion, chopped
2lb red cabbage, shredded
1lb apples, peeled, cored, and sliced
1/2 cup brown sugar
small pinch of ground cloves
1 tsp ground allspice
1 tsp salt
1 2/3 cups red wine
2 tbsp wine vinegar
1 2/3 cups stock (goose, if possible)
Serves 8

Melt butter or dripping in a large flameproof casserole and gently cook bacon and onion until fat runs from bacon and onion is softened. Put in cabbage, pressing down evenly, and cover with layer of apple slices. Add other ingredients, cover tightly and simmer for 2 1/2–3 hours, checking occasionally to see if liquid needs topping up with more water or stock. Taste and adjust seasoning before serving.

Superior Mincemeat

This recipe was found in a tattered London cookbook, inscribed from a Victorian lady to her son's new bride, " ... recommended for beginners ... and not extravagant like Mrs. Beeton". Very easily stirred up, homemade mincemeat needs two to three months maturing, or up to a year for patient connoisseurs. Spices freshly ground in an electric coffee grinder are an incredible improvement to the mixture.

3 1/4 cups raisins
3 cups currants
3 1/4 cups sultanas
2 1/4 cups firmly packed soft brown sugar
about 4 cups tart apples, peeled, cored, and grated
2 cups margarine, chopped
1 cup chopped, candied citrus peel
1/2 cup glacé cherries, halved
scant cup blanched almonds, coarsely chopped
1 1/2 tsp ground nutmeg
1 tsp ground allspice
1/2 tsp ground cloves
grated peel and juice of 2 lemons
1 cup brandy or Irish whiskey
Makes 6 jars

Wash and clean the dried fruit. Mix all ingredients together thoroughly in a large basin or crock, cover tightly, and leave in a cool place for 24 hours. Mix well again and pack tightly into dry, sterilized jars. Cover mincemeat with wax paper or parchment discs, seal jars well, and store in a dark, cool place for at least 2 months before using.

Mont Blanc

This glittering snow mountain of vanilla-flavored chestnut is topped with a glacier of chilled cream and a dusting of dark chocolate. If possible, prepare the Mont Blanc just before serving.

1lb cooked, peeled chestnuts (canned or fresh)
2 cups milk
1 vanilla bean, split
3/4 cup sugar
1 cup heavy cream, whipped
sugar
marsala or rum
grated dark chocolate
Serves 4

Put the chestnuts in a pan with the milk, vanilla bean, and sugar. Cook over low heat until chestnuts are very soft and can be pressed easily through a sieve. Hold the sieve over a large serving platter and push the chestnuts through to fall lightly in a cone-shaped mound. Flavor the softly whipped cream with a little sugar and marsala or rum and spoon on top of the chestnut mountain. Sprinkle grated chocolate over and serve immediately.

Christmas Fruit Cake

A rich treasure of fruit and nuts is well and truly soaked in the spirit of Christmas to make this dark, moist fruit cake. The recipe comes from the west of Ireland where it has been passed down from mother to daughter for several generations.

6½ cups golden raisins
1 cup glacé cherries, halved
½ cup chopped, candied, citrus peel
1 cup Irish whiskey
grated peel and juice of 1 orange
grated peel and juice of 1 lemon
1¼ cups butter
1¼ cups sugar
2½ cups flour
6 eggs
3 apples, finely grated
⅔ cup ground almonds
1 tsp ground cinnamon
½ tsp grated nutmeg
½ tsp ground ginger
¼ tsp ground cloves
½ cup whole walnuts
½ cup whole almonds

In a large bowl, marinate the raisins, cherries, and citrus peel in the whiskey for 2 days, stirring occasionally and keeping fruit well covered in a cool place. Beat butter and sugar together until white and creamy. Beat in eggs and flour alternately. Add soaked fruit, apple, ground almonds, spices, and nuts, stirring well. Pour mixture into a well-greased and lined 10-inch cake pan. Bake in oven preheated to 300°F for the first hour, then reduce heat to 275°F for a further 3 to 4 hours, or until cake is baked through. Cooking time will vary according to type of oven, thickness and shape of cake pan, but it is essential that a low heat is used.

When baked cake is still warm, pierce it all over with a thin skewer and pour whiskey over to soak in. Wrap in fresh waxed paper and aluminum foil and store in a covered tin in a cool, dry place.

Cranberry Chutney

Spicy cranberry chutney makes a change from plain cranberry sauce and a zesty partner for Christmas turkey, as well as for ham and other cold meats. Make extra quantities to give as edible gifts.

6 cups cranberries
1 1/2 cups red wine vinegar
1 generous cup brown sugar
3/4 cup raisins
3/4 cup blanched almonds, chopped
1 tsp ground ginger
1/2 tsp ground cinnamon
1/4 tsp ground cloves
pinch of cayenne pepper
Makes 4 jars

Pick over the cranberries and place with vinegar and brown sugar in a large non-metal or lined pan. Stir over medium heat until cranberries start to pop and release juice. When sugar is dissolved and cranberries are simmering, add raisins, almonds, and spices and bring to slow boil. Stir occasionally until mixture is fairly thick. Taste and add more sugar if chutney seems too sharp. Pour mixture into hot, sterilized jars, allow to cool and seal.

Bûche de Noël

This Yule Log cake has a rolled sponge base and is the centerpiece of French Christmas Eve feasts. Artistic cooks display their talents by decorating the cake with marzipan robins, sugar pine cones, and meringue mushrooms.

3 eggs
scant 1/2 cup superfine sugar
3/4 cup flour
2 tbsp cocoa
superfine sugar for rolling
1/2 cup heavy cream
2 tbsp sugar
few drops vanilla extract
confectioners' sugar or chocolate butter cream to decorate

Prepare an 8 x 12 inch jelly roll pan by greasing and lining with wax paper. Whisk eggs and sugar in the top of a double boiler, or in a bowl set over hot water, until the mixture is pale and thick enough to leave a definite trail. Remove from heat. Sift flour and cocoa together and carefully fold into the egg mixture using a metal spoon. Pour into the prepared pan and spread evenly. Bake in oven preheated to 425°F for 10 minutes, or until mixture is firm to the touch. Turn the cake out onto baking paper or dish towel that has been sprinkled with superfine sugar. Peel off lining paper, trim off crusty edges, and roll cake up with baking paper or tea towel. Cool completely, then unroll carefully and spread with filling of the cream whipped with sugar and vanilla extract.

Reroll cake. Sift over confectioners' sugar to look like snow and decorate with sprig of holly. Alternatively, cover log with chocolate butter cream, score with fork to look like bark, and add decorations.

Gallette des Rois

Properly part of the French Epiphany celebration, this almond-filled pastry known as "Three Kings' Cake" has a bean or tiny ceramic "Infant Jesus" hidden in the filling. The lucky finder is king for the day and chooses his queen. They wear gold paper crowns and can command other revellers to entertain with songs or party pieces.

1lb prepared puff pastry
heaped 1/2 cup ground almonds
scant 1/2 cup superfine sugar
8 tbsp unsalted butter
2 egg yolks
few drops almond extract
1 tbsp rum
beaten egg white

Divide pastry in half and roll into two rounds about 10 inches in diameter. Make filling by mixing ground almonds with the sugar and butter. Work in the egg yolks, almond extract, and rum. Spread the filling on one of the pastry rounds, then press the bean or tiny figure into the almond paste. Moisten the edge of the pastry and cover with the second round, pressing edges well to seal. With the point of a knife, score with wavy lines radiating from the center of the pastry, or with a simple lattice pattern. Brush with some of the beaten egg white and bake in oven preheated to 375°F for about 30 minutes, or until pastry is golden brown. Serve warm.

Frozen Cranberry Parfait

This creamy-pink confection is a refreshing Christmas dessert alternative. Hostess friendly, it can be made a day in advance.

3 cups whole, fresh cranberries
1 cup sugar
grated peel of 1 orange
2 cups crushed graham crackers
6 tbsp butter, melted
1 cup heavy cream
1/4 cup sugar
1/2 tsp vanilla extract
1 cup cream cheese
whipped cream, cranberries, and angelica to decorate
Serves 6-8

Stir cranberries and sugar over low heat until cranberries pop and sugar is dissolved. Add orange rind and allow to cool. Combine finely crushed crackers with melted butter and press into 10-inch round freezer-proof dish. Whip cream and fold in sugar and vanilla essence. Beat cream cheese until soft and fold into whipped cream. Combine cranberries with cream mixture and pour into prepared dish. Freeze until firm. Serve decorated with piped whipped cream, whole cranberries, and angelica cut into holly leaves.

Port Wine Jelly

Elaborate molded desserts were great favorites with the Victorians and this sort of dark wine jelly would have been a star of the Christmas dessert table, swagged in whipped cream and studded with glacé fruits, candied violets, rose petals, and gilded almonds, or whatever luxuries the household might run to.

2½ cups ruby port
½ cup sugar
3 tbsp/45ml lemon juice
½ cup water
1 stick cinnamon, broken
3 tbsp gelatine
whipped cream and decorations
Serves 4

Combine the port, sugar, lemon juice, water, and cinnamon. Remove 6 tablespoons of the liquid and soak gelatine in it. Heat port liquid gently and stir in soaked gelatine liquid; stir until all is dissolved. Pour through wet cheesecloth into a 1½ pint mold which has been rinsed in cold water. Refrigerate to set. Turn out and decorate lavishly.

Christmas Mincemeat Cookies

Use your own homemade or best store-bought mincemeat. These are just the sort of Christmas Eve snacks to leave out for Santa and his helpers. Mincemeat cookies freeze very well for the holiday make-aheads.

1 cup packed mincemeat
boiling water
3 1/2 cups flour
1 tsp salt
1 tsp baking soda
1 tsp ground cinnamon
3/4 cup brown sugar
1/2 lb butter
2 eggs
1 cup raisins
1 cup walnuts, coarsely chopped
Makes approx. 72

Break up mincemeat with a fork and add boiling water a spoonful at a time to make soft mixture, but not soupy. Sift dry ingredients together. Cream butter and sugar together, add eggs and beat in well. Stir in mincemeat, flour mixture, raisins, and nuts. If mixture seems too wet for good dropping consistency, add a little more flour. Drop by spoonfuls on a greased baking sheet and bake in oven preheated to 350°F for about 15 minutes.

Christmas Nougat

This nut-studded sweet is a speciality of the south of France, where it is one of the *treize desserts*; thirteen traditional desserts served after Midnight Mass on Christmas Eve.

3/4 cup shelled pistachio nuts
3/4 cup chopped toasted almonds
3/4 cup honey
1 cup sugar
6 tbsp water
1 egg white, stiffly beaten
3/4 cup red and green glacé cherries, chopped
rice paper

Put the nuts and honey separately into a low oven to warm. Put sugar and water in a pan over low heat and, after sugar is dissolved, cook without stirring until syrup reaches soft crack stage (280°F). Stir in warm honey and bring mixture again to soft crack stage. Remove from heat and pour syrup in thin stream into the beaten egg white, beating constantly. Beat until mixture becomes stiff, fold in warm nuts and cherries and turn into baking tray lined with rice paper. Spread mixture to 1/2-inch thickness and top with a weighted board. Allow to cool and cut into squares.

Date-and-Pecan Roll

These richly textured sweets are sure to please young and old alike. Parcelled in cellophane and tied with bright ribbons, slices of date-and-pecan roll are perfect gifts for fund raisers at Christmas bazaars.

3 cups sugar
1 cup milk
pinch of salt
1 cup chopped dates
1/2 tsp ground cinnamon
grated peel of 1 orange
2 tbsp butter
1 tsp vanilla extract
2 cups chopped pecans

Heat milk, sugar, and salt together over low heat, stirring until sugar is dissolved. Cook to soft ball stage (235°F), then stir in chopped dates, spices, and orange rind. Continue cooking until mixture returns to soft ball temperature, then remove from heat and quickly stir in butter. Allow to cool to lukewarm, then add vanilla extract and beat until mixture thickens. Stir in half the pecans and continue to beat until mixture begins to hold shape. Spread the remaining pecans on a piece of wax paper and form mixture into a roll, pressing pecans evenly into the surface. Allow to set and cut into slices to serve.

Stuffed Dates

Nothing could be easier than these no-cook sweet morsels. This could be a good afternoon project for Santa's younger helpers.

fresh or dried dates
nuts of various sorts
almond paste (see p. 43)
marshmallows, cut up
candied ginger or pineapple
powdered sugar or fine coconut

Carefully open the side of the date and remove stone without spoiling the shape. Stuff center with a piece of nut, almond paste, or any other of the suggested fillings. Press firmly to close and roll in powdered sugar or coconut. If coconut doesn't stick, brush on a little warm jam first.

Homemade Marzipan

This sugared paste of beaten almonds is one of the oldest sweets. In Tudor times it was modelled into fabulous decorations for royal tables, richly colored, or even gilded with beaten gold. Today it is often used to top fruit cake, or formed into little fruit shapes to be artistically colored and served as after-dinner sweets.

1 whole egg
1 egg white
1¾ cups confectioners' sugar, sifted
2 cups ground almonds
2 tsp lemon juice
½ tsp almond extract

Whisk the egg and white with the confectioners' sugar in the top of a double boiler or in a bowl over hot water. Beat until mixture is thick and creamy. Remove from heat, add ground almonds, lemon juice, and almond extract. Knead smooth, adding more confectioners' sugar if necessary. Roll out and cut to shape if covering cake. For marzipan sweets, tint mixture as desired and color details with food colors.

Strawberry Liqueur

This sparkling red liqueur contains all the perfume of ripe summer strawberries, doubly welcome in the depths of winter. Some early planning is required, but the wait is well worth it. Serve in small liqueur glasses or try white wine or champagne cocktails tinged rose with a spoonful of strawberry liqueur in the glass.

ripe strawberries
superfine sugar
vodka

Choose only unblemished strawberries, hull, and pack into large jars, filling to the top. Pour in sugar to fill jars one-third full, shaking down to fill spaces between strawberries. Fill jars to the top with vodka and seal well. Store in a dark, cool place and turn occasionally to help dissolve sugar. Keep for at least 2 months, but 5 to 6 months is better. When ready, strain off the liqueur into clean bottles. The fruit will have given up its color, but is quite tasty to eat.

Christmas Plum Pudding

Proper Christmas pudding should be moist, dark, and rich, bursting with fruit and filling the house with maddening fragrance as it steams away. Traditionally, all members of the family take a turn at stirring the pudding and making a wish. To serve flaming, make sure the spirit used is heated before pouring over the pudding and lighting.

3/4 cup flour
1 1/4 cup fresh breadcrumbs
6oz margarine
1 cup raisins
3/4 cup currants
1 cup grated apple
2/3 cup sugar
scant 1/2 cup chopped, candied citrus peel
1/2 tsp each ground cinnamon, allspice, nutmeg
1/4 tsp ground clove
1/4 cup brandy or whiskey
grated peel and juice of 1 orange
3 eggs
Serves 8-10

Mix ingredients together in order given. Pour into greased, 4 cup basin which has been bottom-lined with a circle of wax paper. Cover tightly with doubled paper and aluminum foil, tie it on and steam for 4 hours. Allow to cool, cover with fresh paper and foil and store in a dry, cool place for at least six weeks. Steam again for 1 1/2 hours before serving.

Brandy Butter

Christmas pudding is unthinkable without its melting rich topping of brandy butter, made in minutes with an electric mixer.

12 tbsp butter
3/4 cup superfine sugar
6 tbsp brandy
grated peel of 1 orange
Makes 3/4 lb

Cream butter and sugar together until light. Beat in brandy a little at a time along with grated orange rind. Spoon into a dish and chill before serving.

Wassail Bowl

The greeting that lives today through Christmas carols comes from the Saxon *was haile*, meaning "good health". This warming drink of hot, spiced ale was also called "lamb's wool" in old England, for obvious reasons.

3 small, hard apples
4 1/2 cups ale
1 stick cinnamon
6 whole cloves
6 allspice berries
2 crushed cardamom pods
2 blades mace
2 strips thin lemon peel
scant 2/3 cup cream
4 tbsp sugar
2 egg yolks

Put the whole apples into a hot oven to roast. Heat ale with spices and peel tied into a piece of cheesecloth. Beat cream, sugar, and egg yolks together. When ale is just starting to simmer, remove spices and peel and whisk in the cream mixture. Keep warm, but do not allow to boil or the mixture will curdle. Serve in large, warmed bowl with roasted apples floating on top.

Christmas Florentines

No-one is sure whether these bejewelled and chocolate-kissed treats are biscuits, cookies, or candy. These specialities glow from the windows of some of the most elegant and expensive *pâtisseries* in the world. Professional-looking Florentines are not difficult to make, but require a little careful handling.

1/2 cup light brown sugar
4 tbsp butter
5 tbsp heavy cream
1 cup whole blanched almonds, chopped
1 cup flaked almonds
heaped 1/2 cup finely chopped red and green glacé cherries
heaped 1/4 cup chopped, candied, orange peel
1/2 cup flour
pinch of salt
8oz semi-sweet chocolate
Makes approx. 48

Combine the sugar, butter, and cream in a heavy pan and stir over heat until mixture comes to the boil and sugar is dissolved. Remove from heat. Toss the nuts, cherries, and orange peel together in the flour to coat evenly and stir all together with the salt into the creamed mixture. Drop small spoonfuls of the mixture onto well-greased baking trays, spacing well apart. Bake in oven preheated to 350°F, until edges are slightly browned. Neaten edges with a plain round cutter or knife, allow to cool slightly, then remove carefully to a wire rack. Melt chocolate and brush a thin coat on the flat side of Florentines to fill any holes. Coat again with chocolate, and when it starts to set, use a fork to mark with wavy lines.

Viennese Christmas Stars

Beautiful star shapes are quick to pipe from a pastry bag with a star nozzle. They can be half-dipped in chocolate or decorated with colored sugars and silver sprinkles.

½ lb butter
⅔ cup confectioners' sugar
1½ tsp vanilla extract
3 cups flour
1 cup cornstarch
Makes approx. 48

Beat butter, sugar, and vanilla extract together until light and fold in remaining ingredients. Using a large star nozzle, pipe mixture into shapes on a greased baking try and bake in oven preheated to 350°F, until golden and slightly brown at edges. Decorate as wished when cool.

Speculaas

Intricate wooden molds are often used for these Dutch Christmas spice cookies, which have spicy holiday counterparts through Germany and Scandinavia. The firm dough is ideal for cutting into all sorts of shapes for Christmas tree decorations.

5 cups all-purpose flour
1 1/2 tsp baking powder
heaped 1/2 cup ground almonds
1 3/4 cups superfine sugar
1 1/2 tsp ground cinnamon
1/2 tsp ground ginger
1/2 tsp ground nutmeg
1/4 tsp ground clove
grated peel of 1 orange
1/2 lb butter
3 eggs, beaten
Makes approx. 48

Sift the flour and baking powder together and add the ground almonds, sugar, spices, and grated peel. Blend in the butter and eggs to make a soft dough, place in a polythene bag, and chill for an hour or more. Press into well-floured molds, if you have them, and turn out, or roll and cut into shapes – angels, bells, stars, etc. Bake on greased trays in oven preheated to 350°F for about 20 minutes or until biscuits are golden brown. Allow to set for a minute or two before removing from baking tray. Cool and decorate.

Glögg

Party-goers may have met versions of this traditional Swedish Christmas drink on the ski slopes. Lethal variations include aquavit or brandy.

2¼ cups port wine
2¼ cups red wine
1 cup water
½ cup sugar
1 stick cinnamon
1 small piece fresh ginger
6 cloves
6 whole cardamoms pods
1 orange, sliced
1 cup brandy
Makes 2½ quarts

Combine port, wine, water, and sugar in a pan over low heat. Tie spices into a piece of cheesecloth and bruise with a mallet. Put spices and orange into the wine mixture and simmer just below boiling point for 15 minutes. Remove spices and pour brandy into the hot mixture. Light very carefully and flame.

Index